for Jean

CLASSICAL AND ROMANTIC P
for Cello and Piano
Arranged by WATSON FORBES

Cello

1. CHANSON TRISTE

REBIKOFF
(1866-1920)

Cello

2. ANDANTINO
(Klavierstücke No. 2)

SCHUBERT
(1797-1828)

3. RONDEAU
(from 'The Fairy Queen')

PURCELL
(1658/9-1695)

4. MENUET

BEETHOVEN
(1770-1827)

5. ROMANCE

(from Piano Concerto in D minor, K466)

MOZART
(1756-1791)

6. POLACCA
(from Brandenburg Concerto No. 1)

J. S. BACH
(1685-1750)

7. BORÉE

HANDEL
(1685-1759)

8. DIVERTIMENTO

HAYDN
(1732-1809)

Cello

9. VITTORIA!

CARISSIMI
(1605-1674)

D. C. al Fine

10. THE DOLL'S LAMENT
(from 'Album for the Young')

TCHAIKOVSKY
(1840-1893)

11. PRELUDE

CHOPIN Op. 28 No.6
(1810-1849)

12. NORWEGIAN DANCE

GRIEG Op. 35 No.2
(1843-1907)

Reproduced and printed by
Halstan & Co. Ltd., Amersham, Bucks., England

D. C. al Fine

Classical and Romantic Pieces for Cello and Piano

Arranged by Watson Forbes

Contents

Oxford University Press

Music Department, Great Clarendon Street, Oxford OX2 6DP

for Jean

CLASSICAL AND ROMANTIC PIECES
for Cello and Piano
Arranged by WATSON FORBES

1. CHANSON TRISTE

REBIKOFF
(1866 - 1920)

Printed in Great Britain

OXFORD UNIVERSITY PRESS, MUSIC DEPARTMENT, GREAT CLARENDON STREET, OXFORD OX2 6DP

2. ANDANTINO

(Klavierstücke No. 2)

SCHUBERT
(1797-1828)

3. RONDEAU

(from 'The Fairy Queen')

PURCELL
(1658/9 - 1695)

4. MENUET

BEETHOVEN
(1770 - 1827)

TRIO

5. ROMANCE

(from Piano Concerto in D minor, K466)

MOZART
(1756 - 1791)

6. POLACCA
(from Brandenburg Concerto No. 1)

J. S. BACH
(1685 - 1750)

7. BORÉE

HANDEL
(1685 - 1759)

8. DIVERTIMENTO

HAYDN
(1732 - 1809)

9. VITTORIA!

CARISSIMI
(1605 - 1674)

10. THE DOLL'S LAMENT

(from *'Album for the Young'*)

TCHAIKOVSKY
(1840 - 1893)

11. PRELUDE

CHOPIN Op. 28 No. 6
(1810 - 1849)

22

12. NORWEGIAN DANCE

GRIEG Op. 35 No. 2
(1843 - 1907)

Reproduced and printed by Halstan & Co. Ltd., Amersham, Bucks., England